MY SIGHT WORD WORKBOOK & READER
LEVEL 2 BOOK 2

Welcome to the **My Sight Word Workbook & Reader Series Level 2**. This series consists of three books **1 to 3**. Your child can complete these books in a timely manner. Each child should be allowed to complete each book at his/her own pace. Each set of books is unique, and the focus is to develop students' sight word recognition skills. The tracing and reading of sight words, and the many activities pre, and posttests, are designed to allow students to master sight word recognition successfully. It is important to note that sight words make up over 70% of all words found in most reading material that students will encounter. Without sight word knowledge, reading will not progress as it should. Knowledge of sight words will allow students to read fluently and comprehend material read. The activities in this text will enhance the teaching and learning process for teachers and students. It is the authors wish that this text will be productive and enjoyable.

THIS SIGHT WORD WORKBOOK AND READER SERIES LEVEL 2 (1 – 3 & THE COMPLETE VOLUME) IS PUBLISHED AND OWNED BY SELLINGTON PUBLISHERS.

My Sight Word Workbook and Reader: Level 2, Book 2 Text Copyright © 2020 by Jacqueline Mitchell.
Cover art and Interior illustrations Copyright © 2020 by Pete McDaniel.

All Rights Reserved. No part of this book may be reproduced in any form or by any electronic or mechanical means including information storage and retrieval systems, without permission in writing from the author.
The only exception is by a reviewer, who may quote short excerpts in a review.

First Edition

ISBN: 978-1-7322038-7-7

This workbook belongs to:

MY SIGHT WORD

WORKBOOK & READER

LEVEL 2 BOOK 2

GRADES K - GRADE 1

JACQUELINE MITCHELL WITH
ILLUSTRATIONS BY PETE MCDANIEL

Conduct sight word pre-test before students have been exposed to the first set of words in the text. Place a check (✓) mark after each word that is correctly recognized.

SIGHT WORD PRETEST

Date: _____

Name: _____
Administrator: _____

SIGHT WORDS	PRE TEST	SIGHT WORDS	PRE TEST
eat		say	
was		new	
she		get	
out		now	
saw		with	
ran		black	
too		brown	
who		there	
our			
TOTAL PERCENTAGE %			
Total Correct			/17

Trace the word "eat". Say the word "eat" aloud.

eat eat eat eat eat

In each sentence below, trace the word: "**eat**".

I like to eat apples.

We eat apples for breakfast.

We eat apples for desert.

We eat apples at school.

We like to eat the red juicy apples.

Write your own sentence using the word: **eat.**

Read the sentences below. Circle the word "eat" in each sentence.

I like to eat apples.
We eat apples for breakfast.
We eat apples for desert.
We eat apples at school.
We like to eat the red juicy apples.

Trace the word "get". Say the word "get" aloud.

get get get get get

In each sentence below, trace the word: "**get**".

Try not to get into trouble today.

Get into the room.

It is time to get into your bed.

You will need to get some rest.

You will get sick.

Write your own sentence using the word: **get**

Read the sentences below. Circle the word "get" in each sentence. Colour the picture below.

Try not to get into trouble today.
Get into the room.
It is time to get into your bed.
You will need to get some rest.
You will get sick.

Trace the word "new". Say the word "new" aloud.

new new new new

 In each sentence below, trace the word: **"new"**.

The new boy is smart.

The new boy can play ball.

The girls is also new.

They are both new.

I like the new girl, she is funny.

The new boy is also funny.

 Write your own sentence using the word: **new.**

Read the sentences below. Circle the word "**new**" in each sentence. Colour the picture below.

The new boy is smart.
The new boy can play ball.
The girl is also new.
They are both new.
I like the new girl, she is funny.
The new boy is also funny.

Trace the word "now". Say the word "now" aloud.

now now now now

 In each sentence below, trace the word: "**now**".

I must go now.

Now is the time for us to talk.

I feel better now.

Now and again they scream.

It is now time to go to sleep.

It is now time to go to school.

 Write your own sentence using the word: **now.**

Read the sentences below. Circle the word "now" in each sentence. Colour the picture below.

I must go now.
Now is the time for us to talk.
I feel better now.
Now and again they scream.
It is now time to go to sleep.
It is now time to go to school.

Trace the word "saw". Say the word "saw" aloud.

saw saw saw saw

 In each sentence below, trace the word: "**saw**".

We saw them in the park.

They saw us too.

They ran when they saw us.

We saw when they ran.

We know that they saw us.

We saw when they stole it.

 Write your own sentence using the word: **saw.**

Read the sentences below. Circle the word "saw" in each sentence.

We saw them in the park.
They saw us too.
They ran when they saw us.
We saw when they ran.
We know that they saw us.
We saw when they stole it.

Trace the word "say". Say the word "say" aloud.

say say say say say

 In each sentence below, trace the word: **"say"**.

We say lots of things.

Sometimes the things we say are not true.

They say they care.

We say nice things to them.

We say good day too.

 Write your own sentence using the word: **say.**

Read the sentences below. Circle the word "**say**" in each sentence. Colour the picture below.

We say lots of things.
Sometimes the things we say are not true.
They say they care.
We say nice things to them.
We say good day too.

Trace the word "she". Say the word "she" aloud.

she she she she she

In each sentence below, trace the word: "**she**".

She is tall.

She is so skinny.

Wow! She is so pretty.

Is she from the country?

Yes. She is from the country.

Will she stay?

Write your own sentence using the word: **she.**

Read the sentences below. Circle the word "she" in each sentence.

She is tall.
She is so skinny.
Wow! She is so pretty.
Is she from the country?
Yes. She is from the country.
Will she stay?

Trace the word "our". Say the word "our" aloud.

our our our our our

In each sentence below, trace the word: **our**.

Our day was good.

All our friends came over.

Our parents were happy.

They helped us plan our party.

Our cake was beautiful.

We played with our toys.

Write your own sentence using the word: **our.**

Read the sentences below. Circle the word "our" in each sentence. Colour the picture below.

Our day was good.
All our friends came over.
Our parents were happy.
They helped us plan our party.
Our cake was beautiful.
We played with our toys.

Trace the word "out". Say the word "out" aloud.

out out out out out

In each sentence below, trace the word: **out**.

Let us go out.

We can go out.

It is fun to go out.

We are happy going out.

When we go out we have lots of fun.

Write your own sentence using the word: **out.**

Read the sentences below. Circle the word "out" in each sentence.

Let us go out.

We can go out.

It is fun to go out.

We are happy going out.

When we go out we have lots of fun.

Trace the word "ran". Say the word "ran" aloud.

ran ran ran ran ran

 In each sentence below, trace the word: "ran".

The boys ran to the swing.

They ran up the hill.

They ran down the hill.

They shouted as they ran

Jack ran down the hill.

They both ran down the hill.

 Write your own sentence using the word: ran.

Read the sentences below. Circle the word "**ran**" in each sentence. Colour the picture below.

The boys ran to the swing.
They ran up the hill.
They ran down the hill.
They shouted as they ran.
Jack ran down the hill.
They both ran down the hill.

Trace the word "too". Say the word "too" aloud.

too too too too too

 In each sentence below, trace the word: "**too**".

There are too many children.

The room is too crowded.

Too many children are there.

There is far too much noise.

Too much noise is not good.

Too little work will get done.

 Write your own sentence using the word: **too.**

Read the sentences below. Circle the word "too" in each sentence. Colour the picture below.

There are two many children.
The room is too crowded.
Too many children are there.
There is far too much noise.
Too much noise is not good.
Too little work will get done.

Trace the word "was". Say the word "was" aloud.

was was was was

In each sentence below, trace the word: **"but"**.

She was not at school today.

She was at home.

It was a rainy day.

It was also windy.

She was ill.

Jan was in bed all day.

Write your own sentence using the word: **was.**

Read the sentences below. Circle the word "was" in each sentence. Colour the picture below.

She was not at school today.
She was at home.
It was a rainy day.
It was also windy.
She was ill.
Jan was in bed all day.

Trace the word "who". Say the word "who" aloud.

who who who who

 In each sentence below, trace the word: "**who**".

Who will go next?

Who will take the basket?

Who will help me?

Who will sweep the floor?

I wonder who will be the first to cry.

 Write your own sentence using the word: **who**.

Read the sentences below. Circle the word "who" in each sentence. Colour the picture below.

Who will go next?
Who will take the basket?
Who will help me?
Who will sweep the floor?
I wonder who will be the first to cry.

Trace the word "with". Say the word "with" aloud.

with with with with

 In each sentence below, trace the word: **"with"**.

I will go with you to the doctor.

You must take the card with you.

You should try pancake with eggs.

Yes, bacon with eggs is also delicious.

 Write your own sentence using the word: **with.**

Read the sentences below. Circle the word "with" in each sentence.

I will go with you to the doctor.
You must take the card with you.
You should try pancake with eggs.
Yes, bacon with eggs is also delicious.

Trace the word "black". Say the word "black" aloud.

black black black black

 In each sentence below, trace the word: "**black**".

Black beans and rice is my favourite meal.

I like the black in the background.

Using black around the border was a good idea.

 Write your own sentence using the word: **black**.

Read the sentences below. Circle the word "black" in each sentence.

Black beans and rice is my favourite meal.

I like the black in the background.

Using black around the border was a good idea.

Trace the word "brown". Say the word "brown" aloud.

brown brown brown

 In each sentence below, trace the word: **brown**.

Mr. Brown lives next door.

The brown dog is barking.

John likes his chicken brown.

Brown stew chicken is delicious.

The cake had on brown icing.

 Write your own sentence using the word: **brown.**

Read the sentences below. Circle the word "brown" in each sentence. Colour the picture below.

Mr. Brown lives next door.
The brown dog is barking.
John likes his chicken brown.
Brown stew chicken is delicious.
The cake had on brown icing.

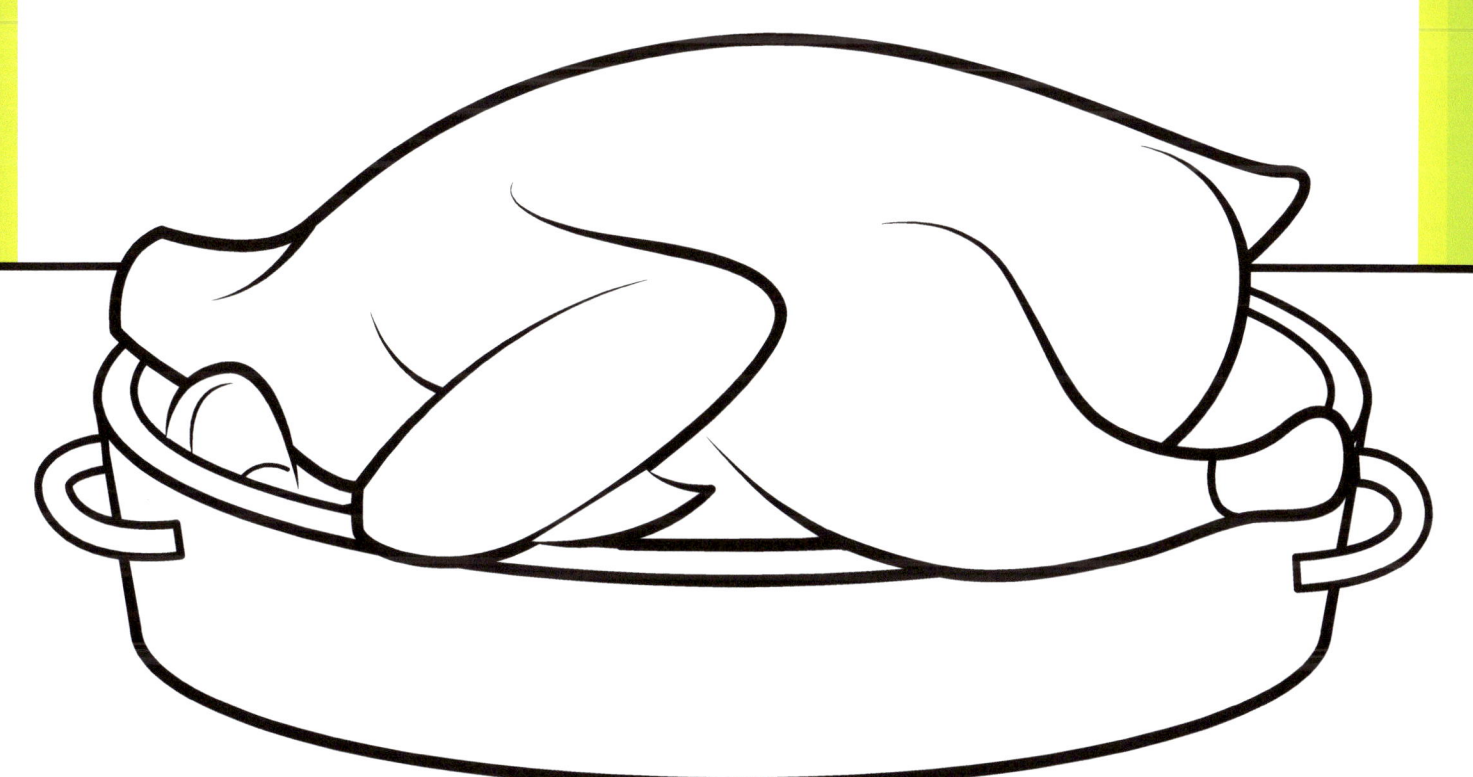

Trace the word "there". Say the word "there" aloud.

there there there there there

 In each sentence below, trace the word: "**there**".

There are three green bottles on the table.

Look over there on the table.

The apples are over there on the table.

Write your own sentence using the word: **there.**

Read the sentences below. Circle the word "**what**" in each sentence.

There are three green bottles on the table.
Look over there on the table.
The apples are over there on the table.

Fill in the missing letters in the sight words below. Write the word correctly in the space provided then pronounce each word.

1. e___t — eat
2. w___s — was
3. s___e — she
4. o___t — out
5. s___w — saw
6. ___o___ — too
7. wh___ — who
8. o___r — our
9. s___y — say
10. n___w — new
11. ge___ — get
12. n___w — now
13. r___n — ran
14. w___th — with
15. bl___ck — black
16. br___wn — brown
17. th___re — there

Write the words from the word box in the correct shapes. Say each word out loud.

eat now get was with black
she new our say brown there
out who ran too saw

a e i o u and sometimes **y** are vowels. Circle the vowels in the words below. How many vowels are in each word? Write the answer in the space provided beside each word.

eat _____

was _____

she _____

out _____

saw _____

ran _____

too _____

who _____

our _____

say _____

new _____

get _____

now _____

with _____

black _____

brown _____

there _____

Match the words below on the left to the correct ones on the right. One has been done for you.

eat	out
was	she
now	with
get	eat
new	was
too	get
out	our
ran	black
saw	new
say	brown
who	there
she	now
our	too
with	ran
black	who
brown	saw
there	say

Colour the picture below, and then use the space below to write about the picture.

Find the words in the puzzle.

```
e s h e x u u o b
a z p t g e t u l
t o q h n e w r a
w u s e t o o w c
a t a r n o w w k
s b w e o t m h w
s a y r a n u o n
b r o w n w i t h
```

1. eat
2. was
3. she
4. out
5. saw
6. ran
7. too
8. who
9. our
10. say
11. new
12. get
13. now
14. with
15. black
16. brown
17. there

Flash cards:: Cut cards and paste them on cartridge paper or cardboard. Allow students to use these cards in board games and matching activities to help in memorizing words.

eat	she
saw	too
our	new

was	out
ran	who
say	get

now	with
black	brown

there

Read the sentences below. Find the words from the word box in each sentence below and circle them.

too now our was she who say out
saw get new ran eat

I like to eat apples.

We get apples at school. Mom told us not to get into trouble today.

The new boy at school can play ball. The new boy is also funny.

It is now time to go to school.

We saw them in the park. They ran when they saw us.

We say nice things to them.

Wow! She is so pretty. Is she from the country? Yes. She is from the country.

Read the sentences below. Find the words from the word box in each sentence below and circle them.

too	now	our	was	she	who	say	out
saw	get	new	ran	eat			

Let us go out in the yard and play.

All our friends came over. They helped us plan our party. Our day was good.

It is fun to go out and play.

The boys ran to the swing. They shouted as they ran.

There are too many children.

Jan was in bed all day.

She did not come out to play.

Conduct sight word post-test after students have been exposed to the first set of words in the text. Words that were incorrectly recognized should be reviewed and post test administered again where necessary. Place a check (✓) mark beside each word that is correctly recognized.

SIGHT WORD POST TEST

Date: _____

Name: _____
Administrator: _____

SIGHT WORDS	POST TEST	SIGHT WORDS	POST TEST
eat		say	
was		new	
she		get	
out		now	
saw		with	
ran		black	
too		brown	
who		there	
our			
TOTAL PERCENTAGE %			
Total Correct			/17

www.ingramcontent.com/pod-product-compliance
Lightning Source LLC
Chambersburg PA
CBHW042122040426
42450CB00002B/37